IN
RETREAT

America's Withdrawal
from the Middle East

[For a list of books published under the auspices of the
WORKING GROUP ON ISLAMISM AND THE INTERNATIONAL ORDER,
please see page 61.]

HERBERT & JANE DWIGHT WORKING GROUP ON ISLAMISM AND THE INTERNATIONAL ORDER

ESSAY SERIES: THE GREAT UNRAVELING: THE REMAKING OF THE MIDDLE EAST

IN
RETREAT

America's Withdrawal
from the Middle East

Russell A. Berman

HOOVER INSTITUTION PRESS
Stanford University   Stanford, California

www.hoover.org

Hoover Institution Press Publication No. 646

Hoover Institution at Leland Stanford Junior University, Stanford, California, 94305-6010

First printing 2014
21 20 19 18 17 16 15 14   9 8 7 6 5 4 3 2 1

Manufactured in the United States of America

The paper used in this publication meets the minimum requirements of the American National Standard for Information Sciences— Permanence of Paper for Printed Library Materials, ANSI/NISO Z39.48-1992. ⊗

Cataloging-in-Publication Data is available from the Library of Congress.
ISBN 978-0-8179-1725-8 (pbk.: alk. paper)
ISBN 978-0-8179-1726-5 (epub)
ISBN 978-0-8179-1727-2 (mobi)
ISBN 978-0-8179-1728-9 (PDF)

The Hoover Institution gratefully acknowledges the following individuals and foundations for their significant support of the

HERBERT AND JANE DWIGHT WORKING GROUP ON ISLAMISM AND THE INTERNATIONAL ORDER:

Herbert and Jane Dwight

Beall Family Foundation

Stephen Bechtel Foundation

Lynde and Harry Bradley Foundation

Mr. and Mrs. Clayton W. Frye Jr.

Lakeside Foundation

CONTENTS

The Great Unraveling:
The Remaking of the Middle East

IT'S A MANTRA, but it is also true: the Middle East is being unmade and remade. The autocracies that gave so many of these states the appearance of stability are gone, their dreaded rulers dispatched to prison or exile or cut down by young people who had yearned for the end of the despotisms. These autocracies were large prisons, and in 2011, a storm overtook that stagnant world. The spectacle wasn't pretty, but prison riots never are. In the Fertile Crescent, the work of the colonial cartographers—Gertrude Bell, Winston Churchill, and Georges Clemenceau— are in play as they have never been before. Arab nationalists were given to lamenting that they lived in nation-states "invented" by Western powers in the aftermath of the Great War. Now, a century later, with the ground burning in Lebanon, Syria, and Iraq and the religious sects at war, not even the most ardent nationalists can be sure that they can put in place anything better than the old order.

Men get used to the troubles they know, and the Greater Middle East seems fated for grief and breakdown. Outside powers approach it with dread; merciless political contenders have the run of it. There is swagger in Iran and a belief that the radical theocracy can bully its rivals into submission. There was a period when the United States provided a modicum of order in these Middle Eastern lands. But pleading fatigue, and financial scarcity at home, we have all but announced the end of that stewardship. We are poorer for that abdication, and the Middle East is thus left to the mercy of predators of every kind.

We asked a number of authors to give this spectacle of disorder their best try. We imposed no rules on them, as we were sure their essays would take us close to the sources of the malady.

FOUAD AJAMI
Senior Fellow, Hoover Institution—
Cochairman, Herbert and Jane Dwight Working Group
on Islamism and the International Order

CHARLES HILL
Distinguished Fellow of the Brady-Johnson Program
in Grand Strategy at Yale University;
Research Fellow, Hoover Institution—
Cochairman, Herbert and Jane Dwight Working Group
on Islamism and the International Order

In Retreat

America's Withdrawal from the Middle East

RUSSELL A. BERMAN

NOT LONG AGO, it seemed that the Middle East would be reborn in the spirit of the Arab Spring. The liberal aspirations that suddenly erupted across the region promised to overthrow despots, end repression, and remake the future, while partaking of the culture of innovation through social media that has come to mark a new global generation. Hopes for bright opportunities pointed to profound transformations.

But in response to those glowing aspirations, a new repression has set in, a reactionary turn against the prospects for freedom and free societies. Much of this has indigenous roots; there were always many powerful opponents to change, and the revolution gave way to counterrevolution and

1

bloodshed. Yet there is also an international context, defined especially by the policies of the one state that had survived the Cold War as the single superpower: the United States. Of course US policies have never fully dictated the vicissitudes of the region, but they have had great influence for decades. So when, in the wake of the 2008 US presidential elections, new messages began to emerge from Washington, the consequences were significant. Instead of the Bush administration's robust effort to remake the Middle East, the Obama administration has pursued a generalized reduction of the American footprint. A grand retreat has begun, and the reduction of the US commitment has, in turn, set off a wave of repercussions. What the ultimate outcome of this retreat will be we cannot predict, nor can we know whether the next administration will continue to withdraw from a region that the US has regarded as central to its international security strategy for decades.

We can, however, know what the US has been doing, just as we can examine what American leaders have been saying with regard to the Middle East and its future. Such an examination can help us understand what motivates the retreat, how much it is a choice of the Obama administration, and how much it is rooted in deeper American cultural leanings that could outlast the administration. The departure from the Middle East involves some powerful shifts in the worldview of Americans in general and parts of the policy-making elite in particular with regard to America's role in the world. It is not only about changing evaluations about this specific corner of the globe; it also reflects predispositions to retreat from politics altogether, to retreat from the burden of leadership, and to retreat from the advocacy for democracy. Each of these retreats deserves scrutiny.

RETREAT FROM POLITICS

To understand America's retreat from the Middle East, one has to recognize how it is, at least in part, a reflection of the degradation of politics in general, which characterizes our culture in the first decades of the twenty-first century. The American departure from a part of the world in which it has provided security and stability for more than a half-century is not only a limited strategic decision—although it certainly does include specific geopolitical miscalculations in Washington. It is also a much broader phenomenon: a secular diminishment of politics, a disdain for politicians and the possibilities of domestic civic life. This renunciation of political vision has translated into a reduction of foreign-policy ambitions, of which the exit from the Middle East is a prime example. The generalized flight from politics, which has supported an isolationist reorientation of the American mind, has multiple causes, some profound, rooted deeply in the shifts of post-Cold War culture, while some are the direct effect of the character of the Obama administration. The extensive significance of this withdrawal from the world, isolationism as a particular form of depoliticization, becomes clear by first stepping back briefly to consider the potentials of politics, in general, as well as the sources of antipolitical sentiment.

Politics involves collaboration, working together to formulate strategies through conflict and compromise and then to participate in their execution. Politics entails partnerships—alliances, allies, coalitions, caucuses—where deliberation and argument play out in order to reach decisions. It's no wonder that politics, on one level, is tied closely to rhetoric: politicians have to persuade, and once the persuasion and negotiation conclude by achieving a program, action can be taken to carry it out. The crux of politics is the deliberation, whether among free citizens within a state or among representatives of sovereign states in international affairs.

Yet that ideal of a deliberative politics, central to the thinking of the founders of the American republic who built on the classical traditions of antiquity, has always faced challenges from alternative accounts of the political for which the concerted action of citizens did not count for much. For Marxists and other proponents of the social state, the political life of the citizenry pales in significance, since they view it as merely a secondary reflection of the allegedly more profound reality of the economy. In this version, politicians are only agents, shadow boxers, or figureheads, standing in for the genuine reality of hidden economic forces; political speech is, so the adherents of this viewpoint argue, a mere camouflage of avaricious ulterior motives. Such fascination with hidden agenda explains why this line of thinking often devolves into conspiracy theories with simplistic narratives of innocent victims and hidden powers of evil. Through fairy tales like this and, more generally though, due to the pull toward the primacy of the economy, such approaches threaten to undermine the public sphere and contribute to forms of depoliticization, and they therefore reduce the capacity of the community of citizens to pursue its goals through political action.

Meanwhile, however, the republican tradition of civic virtue faces more sophisticated criticism from another camp that emphasizes politics as the instrumental capacity to exercise power and impose control. Niccolò Machiavelli was the first prominent proponent of the primacy of power, followed by Friedrich Nietzsche and then Max Weber, who defined the state in terms of its claim to hold a monopoly on the exercise of legitimate violence. In this tradition, politics is not about an independent sphere of deliberation in which autonomous citizens pursue freedom;

rather, it is only a matter of assuring that the state can wield violence most effectively. The fact of state power is what matters, not the character of political life (i.e., whether it is democratic or dictatorial). This instrumentalism leads directly to the deeply non-Marxist implication of the viewpoint expounded by a leading Communist politician of the twentieth century, Mao Tse-tung, the claim that power grows out of the barrel of a gun. This fetishism of violence has had its own bloody history in parts of the anti-colonial movements, in the killing fields of Cambodia, in the tyrants of the developing world, and in the multiple ideologies of terrorism that have besieged the planet in recent decades. What links these various examples is not only the ease with which radical movements have been prepared to shed blood in pursuit of their goals, but, even more fundamentally, the primary focus on the tools of power, the guns out of which power allegedly grows. The instruments and technologies through which the state exercises power displace consideration of the genuine values and goals that politics might pursue. The greater the focus on the tools and

7

the weapons, the smaller the importance of political debate. Nineteenth-century German Chancellor Otto von Bismarck would have endorsed this viewpoint with his insistence that "blood and iron" were the means with which to pursue national goals, not political speeches or parliamentary debates.

The art of politics, the capacity to search for compromise and build cooperation, has always faced threats from these twin antipolitical tendencies: economic reductionism and instrumentalist violence. These forms of depoliticization undermine democracy. Yet in contemporary American culture, one cannot help but note a similar antipolitical mood, a degradation of public deliberation, whether it is gridlocked in Congress or polarized on the radio. A retreat from politics mars contemporary American culture, magnified by the specific character of the Obama administration, and this provides part of the explanation of the great American retreat from a political role in the Middle East. Giving up on politics, we, as a culture, are giving up on political ambitions, including the capacity to act strategically in the world and, especially, the Middle

East. One wonders whether today's Washington can envision any grand strategy, let alone carry it out.

It was not always so. Leaving aside the long history of American achievements since the end of the Second World War, one can cite examples of recent success, including the extraordinary accomplishments of US policy in bringing the Cold War to an end. American diplomacy played an indispensable role in redesigning a Europe in a way that has led to the European Union and a peaceful continent. Whatever the fiscal problems within the euro zone, the EU itself has proven an enormous success when measured against what preceded it, a divided Europe, with Russian troops and weapons in the middle of Germany. Bringing the Cold War to an end was a victory of American foreign policy during the Republican administration of George H. W. Bush, and ending the bloodshed in the Balkans represented a comparable achievement of US diplomacy during the Democratic administration of Bill Clinton. Not that long ago, then, America engaged robustly in the world in ways that contributed indisputably to the good. Without that

American commitment to political engagement, the map of Europe might look quite different today, and the lands of the former Yugoslavia might still be seething with violence.

An inclination to retreat from an engaged foreign policy already began to emerge during the first months of the George W. Bush presidency, with its initial resistance to the nation-building policies associated with its predecessor. Yet in the wake of the terrorist attacks of September 11, 2001, the prosecution of the war on terror pulled the US into the Middle East and Central Asia, redefining foreign-policy goals toward the ambitious project to spread democracy. While this policy turn resulted primarily from the terrorist attacks and the pursuit of Al Qaeda, it is important to note how the democracy agenda also displayed a striking continuity with the emphasis on human rights from the Clinton years as well as from the Republican legacy of Ronald Reagan, all of which based foreign-policy goals on understanding American values as having universal validity.

At first, those ambitions seemed bold but certainly credible in the light of recent historical experience. The dictatorships of Communist Eastern Europe had collapsed with little violence (except in the sorry case of Romania), and it could seem plausible that a similar democratic wave would sweep triumphantly, and peacefully, through the Arab world in the wake of the toppling of Saddam Hussein. (Nor was that aspiration fully wrong, since, with some delay, the Arab Spring would follow and unsettle the old order of Middle East dictators. But it would quickly involve significant violence, and the response from Obama's Washington would be quite different, much more hesitant and confused, than the Bush administration's unambiguous support for the transformation of Eastern Europe.) The optimistic illusion that the changes in the Arab world would take place as smoothly as those in the post-Communist world after 1989 may have contributed to the catastrophic insufficiency of political postwar planning by the US as to how to rebuild Iraq after the fall of Saddam. At the very apex of the American victory, the moment of military victory in Baghdad, the limits of American political thinking became apparent. We could topple the dictator, but we had no plans to help the nation rebuild, especially when the extent of devastation caused by the years of Baathist rule became apparent.

The aspiration to define victory in Iraq exclusively in terms of the use of military force, the program of "shock and awe," was itself symptomatic of a reluctance to give the political sphere its due. To imagine that American influence could rely exclusively on the technologies of war or, for that matter, on economic largesse in terms of foreign aid is to miss the importance of political institutions—building the partnerships, alliances, and coalitions of sovereign states with commitments to shared goals. The history of the past years in both Iraq and Afghanistan has shown the Obama administration's repeated unwillingness to build those alliances through the compromises that define the very nature of politics. It let the negotiations with Iraq collapse over a status of forces agreement by refraining from making any serious political effort to reach a compromise. It has similarly failed to manage the relationship with Afghanistan President Hamid Karzai. In each case, the political failure set the stage for American withdrawal. Moreover, the administration's consistent aversion to political accomplishment in the foreign-policy arena helps explain the curious character of Hillary Clinton's tenure as secretary of state, marked by much frenetic travel that led to no achievements of note. No chief American diplomat has ever flown so far to do so little.

The US experiences in Afghanistan and Iraq and the US responses to Iran and Syria all have their own character and deserve detailed study. Yet we should not forget the forest for the trees: a long-term process has been unfolding in recent years, marked by a devaluation of politics and an amplified reliance on technology. Consider this trajectory of American foreign policy: after the unification of a democratic Europe, the opposition to genocide in the Balkans, and vocal advocacy for human rights, followed by the democracy agenda of the Bush years, Obama's Washington has turned to an ever-shrinking engagement, symbolically represented by the deployment of the weapons system that most symbolizes the absence of a human element, drone warfare. No drone ever won hearts and minds. Yet it is drone technology that has come to define US presence in the region, in a way the president explicitly endorsed in his notorious remark that "I'm really good at killing people," as reported by Mark Halperin and John Heilemann in their account of the 2012 election, *Double Down.*

The aversion to politics is especially clear in the grand trade-off the Obama administration has pursued, rejecting regime change in order to pursue arms control: political form matters less than the instruments of war. Recall how the administration twice faced moments when popular democratic movements have burgeoned into significant threats to dictatorial regimes hostile to the United States: the Green Movement in Iran in 2009 and the beginning of the revolution in Syria in 2011. Yet with regard to Iran and Syria, the Obama administration provided nothing more than meager verbal support for the democratic opposition; and it failed to subject the regimes to any noticeable pressure to refrain from crushing their critics. For the Obama administration, a political outcome that would have entailed regime change has always been too frightening to pursue. In the end, it has staked its own reputation on the durability of the mullahs in Tehran and the House of Assad in Damascus. The call for democracy, a leitmotif in US foreign policy from Woodrow Wilson to George W. Bush, has been silenced by the Obama administration.

Instead of democracy, Washington has focused exclusively on managing weapons technology. Arms control, especially halting the proliferation of nuclear arms, is a vital and legitimate component of efforts to prevent catastrophic warfare. Yet in the wake of the revelation of the clandestine talks with Iran that led to the interim agreement, the Joint Plan of Action, it became clear the Obama administration had willingly sacrificed democratic politics in Syria in order to try to limit Iranian weaponry. It has also viewed drawing the Iranian regime into arms control negotiations as preferable to supporting the protest movement against the Iranian regime. As of this writing, the outcome of those negotiations remains quite uncertain, and doubts are rising as to whether Iran will credibly curtail its drive for a nuclear bomb. Similarly the agreement to eliminate Syria's capacity to produce chemical weapons may turn out to be unverifiable, and it is evident that Damascus is dragging its feet in turning over its arsenal.

It is painfully clear that Washington has paid a price for these negotiations—not in Iran, but in Syria. While the Iran negotiations were under way in secret, the civil war in Syria was raging, and the Bashar al-Assad regime was carrying out gas warfare, prohibited by international law and shunned by the civilized world. As long as the casualties from these attacks remained relatively limited—in the tens and twenties—the US chose to say as little as possible and do nothing: it even denied requests from regime opponents to equip them with gas masks and anti-sarin injection kits. Washington took every opportunity to minimize its involvement in Syria and refrain from significant opposition to Assad precisely in order to shelter the negotiations with Iran, Assad's protector. Had the US instead protested vigorously against the use of gas, it apparently believed that the negotiations with Iran might be jeopardized. Instead, in remarks made in Stockholm, the president spoke in a way that signaled that gas warfare below a certain threshold could be tolerated. In his words, "a whole bunch" of chemical weapons would have to be used before he would reconsider reacting to Assad's gas warfare. The initial victims of Assad's repeated attacks were, evidently, sacrificed to the American realpolitik of pursuing the arms control negotiations with Iran, and the success of that realism remains unclear.

Not until the attack of August 21, 2013, which claimed more than 1,400 victims, did Obama speak out decisively against the use of gas. Finally the "red line" he had drawn earlier had been crossed in a way that demanded a response. Yet he abruptly backed down, and the damage to his credibility was enormous because of the confusion and mixed messages that characterized Washington's response. That profound diminishment of the prestige of the US president is also part of the retreat from politics.

The failure of politics: in Iraq the administration let the negotiations to come to a status of forces agreement collapse, and in Afghanistan the prospect of an American role in the future is in doubt. Without any regional political ambitions, the US is clearing out, and the regional actors know it. That inability to carry out politics, however, reflects the priority of the administration's disregard to questions of rights, democracy, or political substance. We are witnessing the transformation of foreign policy from the pursuit of core democratic values into an instrumentalist reasoning which, in terms of weapons reduction, has yet to show any success. Meanwhile the US, once the undisputed leader of the West, is ceding the region to competitors and enemies. At this point, the antipolitical inclinations of the administration and our culture, veering toward isolationism, turn into an explicit abdication of leadership.

RETREAT FROM LEADERSHIP

As much as politics requires collaboration among multiple participants, it also demands leadership. The leader takes initial steps to set a process in motion. Without leadership, politics runs the risk of devolving into inertia and bureaucracy. This holds as much in a town-hall meeting as it does in the halls of Congress, and there is an analogous necessity of leadership in international relations. International challenges abound, but they will not be addressed unless some nation or nations first direct attention to them. The strongest and wealthiest nations are great powers, and these are the international actors with the greatest responsibility because they have the potential to influence the outcomes most effectively. To act as a great power requires a generous vision that surpasses one's narrowest and most self-interested ambitions by taking into consideration the greater good of the international system. A great power should not pursue its parochial interests selfishly. However, when a great power refrains from acting in the international interest and chooses, instead, not to act at all, it betrays its responsibility to the world.

The international order that has prevailed in the wider Middle East for nearly seventy years is unraveling, leading potentially to a band of failed states stretching from Afghanistan through Syria and Egypt to Libya and Algeria. The explanations are multiple, including distinctly indigenous causes as well as broadly international developments: the spiraling effects of the end of the Cold War and, related to that, the rise of Islamist militancy and its Shiite corollary, the fifth columns of the Iranian revolution. Yet the rapidity with which the unraveling is proceeding can only be explained by America's grand retreat: as the Obama administration retreats from politics, it has also been renouncing traditional American claims on leadership. Without the international leadership that only Washington could provide, the center does not hold and things fall apart across the Middle East.

Hostility to American leadership has a long history in many parts of the world. It erupted most notoriously in the wave of anti-Americanism in Western Europe during the years of the George W. Bush administration. Yet of interest here is something different: not the international aversion to American leadership but the American aversion to exercising leadership. Fundamentally isolationist, it involves a retreat from responsibility through a reluctance to lead. This predisposition reflects underlying changes in US education and culture: a misunderstanding of an equality of rights as necessarily inimical to differences in ability and power and a widespread suspicion of elites, be they elites of knowledge, wealth, or authority. In the international system, this culture of antielitism translates into a refusal to act as a leader.

This hostility to leading distinctly defines the Obama presidency and the president's personal style. Individuals, especially those in positions of great power, can play decisive roles in history. Yet the president generally appears to prefer to hand off responsibilities to others. He has refrained from extensive activism with Congress where he might have steered legislative processes, and he has chosen to deflect criticism by repeatedly claiming that he has not been informed about key issues, rather than, as leader, taking ultimate responsibility: the politicization of the IRS, the scope of NSA surveillance, or the troubled roll-out of the health-care website. His habit of evading responsibility demonstrates a resistance on his part to assume the burden of leadership. This particular aspect of presidential character and the general antipathy toward leaders and elites afoot in the culture help contextualize the retreat from American leadership in the Middle East.

Of course it is not only Obama's character that is at stake but also his political inclinations. He recoils from the notion that the US should pursue a transformative agenda abroad. He has no plans to change the world (despite the allegations of his radicalism), in contrast to the advocacy for regime change and democracy that marked the previous administration. That might suggest, unexpectedly, a kind of conservatism in Obama's geopolitical sensibility, and that is partly correct: he does not want to see regimes toppled, especially not dictatorial ones. Yet classically conservative foreign policies might pursue a determined maintenance of the status quo, and that is hardly the hallmark of the Obama years, defined instead in terms of a withdrawal, a diminishment of American influence, and an instinct to minimize any projection of US power abroad. It is true he attributes this quietism to the war-weariness of the American public, but that public opinion is also, to a large extent, of his own making, since he has repeatedly refused to use his bully pulpit to make the strong case for American security initiatives, whether with regard to the war in Afghanistan or the NSA surveillance. If the president does not explain them convincingly, the public withholds its support. In the arena of public opinion formation, too, the president has refrained from leading.

The refusal of leadership and the attendant diminishment of the role of the US in the Middle East defines a series of events in the past years, from the belated and halfhearted role the US played in Libya, notorious as the strategy of leading from behind (in other words, ceding leadership to others while covering the costs), to the decision to refrain from engagement in Syria. In the first case, Washington handed over the pride of place in defining the goals of the mission to France and the United Kingdom; in the latter case, Washington made way for Russia to assume the key responsibility. In Libya, the consequences include ongoing disorder and a continued threat of terrorist violence, coupled with governmental instability; in Syria, even the control of chemical weapons has not yet been resolved, nor is there any verifiable guarantee the chemical weapons production capacity has been fully dismantled, while the killing continues and refugees number in the millions.

The retreat from leadership is in fact programmatic, as was made clear in a series of statements by the president: the Cairo address on June 4, 2009, in which the still-new president tried to reach out to the Muslim world; the August 31 speech on Syria, in the wake of the mass killings of August 21 due to the Assad regime's use of gas warfare and for which the president seemed to threaten a military response; and the follow-up speech on September 10, in which the president abruptly ratcheted down the threat. Reading these three documents closely provides insights into the fundamental orientations of the administration's foreign-policy vision.

Building on promises from his election campaign and inaugural address, President Obama delivered the speech titled "A New Beginning" in the main hall of Cairo University; Al-Azhar University cosponsored the event. The address assumed the policies of the Bush administration had damaged the estimation of the US in Muslim eyes, even though President Bush had taken pains to distinguish scrupulously between the Muslim religion and the military adversaries in Afghanistan, Iraq, and the war on terror. The vague breadth of the addressee—the Muslim world in general—lent the talk an ethereal character. It opens with religious gestures, and it concludes with explicit quotations from the Koran, the Talmud, and the Bible. While it touches on a range of policy issues, from the Israeli-Palestinian conflict to women's rights, it remains only at a very high level of generality. It lacks specificity precisely because its addressee is so vague: all the world's Muslims. In retrospect this was indeed a bizarre episode: imagine a head of any state, let alone a superpower, delivering a major speech directed to the world's Catholics or Jews, Buddhists or Hindus.

The ostensible goal of the speech was to mollify the presumed animosity of the audience toward the US. To achieve this goal, however, the president specifically excluded reference to concrete accomplishments of American policy. He might, for example, have mentioned the decades of considerable aid the US had provided to Egypt and emphasized the close ties between the two countries. Alternatively he might have referenced the role the US military had played in halting the genocide of the Bosnian Muslims during the Balkan War. Yet both were curiously omitted—or perhaps not curiously at all, since Bosnia brings to mind US military intervention, just as the ties to Egypt involve significant military cooperation and arms support. That sort of hard power is precisely what President Obama has not wanted to project, even if, as in the Balkans case, it had been deployed in the service of stopping genocide. (Only a few years later, he would refrain from providing military support to halt mass killings in Syria.)

Instead of appealing to his audience by invoking the accomplishments of American strength, the president describes America's future presence in the region as weak and therefore unthreatening. Instead of recalling what the US achieved in the Balkans, the president emphasizes only that the US would depart from the Middle East as rapidly as possible. Despite the penumbra of good feeling the speech was intended to project through the appeals to religious sentiment, the core message articulated at Cairo University was that the US would soon be gone. It would no longer represent a significant power in the Middle East, and it should not be counted on to provide leadership or security. Somehow this self-denigration was supposed to elicit respect.

Thus the audience in Cairo could hear the American president promise the US has no desire to keep forces in Afghanistan. "Make no mistake: we do not want to keep our troops in Afghanistan. We seek no military bases there. It is agonizing for America to lose our young men and women. It is costly and politically difficult to continue this conflict. We would gladly bring every single one of our troops home if we could be confident that there were not violent extremists in Afghanistan and Pakistan determined to kill as many Americans as they possibly can. But that is not yet the case." Of course he provides a justification for the military engagement in Afghanistan, the war on terror. Yet the relevant message is not the ex post facto rationale for the intervention but the prospective vision of the American departure. An alternative message might have been for the president to underscore the intractability of the problem of terrorism, how terrorism is inimical to stable societies, and why Muslims could count on continued US support in defending the rule of law. However, that was the road not taken in this speech which all but sounds retreat.

The president similarly promised a rapid abandonment of any American presence in Iraq, disguising this renunciation of leadership as a form of "responsibility": "Today, America has a dual responsibility: to help Iraq forge a better future—and to leave Iraq to Iraqis. I have made it clear to the Iraqi people that we pursue no bases, and no claim on their territory or resources. Iraq's sovereignty is its own." The president also gestured toward a future partnership with Iraq in terms of security and economic development. Such plans might have sounded promising in theory, but in practice, the Obama administration would let negotiations with Baghdad founder over the status of forces agreement, and the US would leave Iraq, letting it slide further into the orbit of Iranian influence and continued sectarian strife.

In his Cairo speech, President Obama advertised the post-American future of the region. That vision, however, had to do with more than questions of stationing troops; it also called into question the underlying idealistic rationale for the American presence, the motivating value of the Bush presidency: democracy. The Cairo speech was a watershed not because of its character as an appeal to Muslims but because it represented an American abdication of its leadership role of democracy. To distance himself from his predecessor, President Obama had to distance himself from the vision of political change: "I know there has been controversy about the promotion of democracy in recent years, and much of this controversy is connected to the war in Iraq. So let me be clear: no system of government can or should be imposed upon one nation by any other."

President Obama could not have been more explicit: no dictator should ever again feel threatened that the US will push for regime change. This is a stark and pessimistic vision, profoundly foreign to the sense of progress in human affairs that has defined American political culture from Woodrow Wilson and Franklin D. Roosevelt to Reagan and Bush, an obligation to promote the spread of freedom and democracy. Still, the president cannot let go of this credo fully, but his argument in the Cairo speech is tortured and contradictory. When he states that the promise not to impose a form of government from the outside "does not lessen my commitment, however, to governments that reflect the will of the people," he confesses his sympathy for democracies but promises no support in their defense. The matter grows complicated, however, when he proceeds to suggest that cultural diversity may not always lead to democratic outcomes. "Each nation gives life to this principle in its own way, grounded in the traditions of its own people. America does not presume to know what is best for everyone, just as we would not presume to pick the outcome of a peaceful election." That statement amplifies the commitment against intervention: no matter how the people's will finds expression in a political form, the US will refrain from judging the outcomes because he presumes that nations are separated by fundamental cultural differences in their traditions. Nations are too different ever to warrant judgment.

The Cairo speech was ultimately an announcement that the US would henceforth refrain from providing leadership, military or otherwise, in the region. Leadership would therefore have to come from elsewhere, which explains the remarkable turn of phrase at the conclusion of the speech. For a president who, domestically, has sometimes been criticized for not taking religion seriously enough, it is noteworthy that he ends with these words: "The people of the world can live together in peace. We know that is God's vision. Now, that must be our work here on Earth. Thank you. And may God's peace be upon you." It is unthinkable that he would deliver an address in the US claiming that he is guided by "God's vision." He does so in Cairo, however, because he conceives of the speech not as a substantive policy address but as an outreach to a population defined in religious terms. Still, his fundamental quietism rings through. Pursuing "God's vision," for the president, is not an activist agenda to realize certain substantive values or to create a heaven on earth. "God's vision" involves no transformation, no improvement of the world. Instead it only implies maintaining the status quo among peoples with different cultures, and also among states with different political cultures.

President Obama had hoped to end conflict in the region by putting a cap on the wars in Afghanistan and Iraq. After Cairo, however, the unraveling and turmoil of the following years soon eclipsed his optimism. The Iranian election that took place barely a week after the Cairo address set off the "Green Movement," with masses of protesters who faced brutal government assaults. The war in Libya would follow, leading to an instability that continues to today, with ramifications that have contributed to the fighting in Mali and the Central African Republic. During the same four years, Egypt faced profound shocks twice, first with the overthrow of Hosni Mubarak, whom the US chose to abandon, and then the ousting of his successor, Mohamed Morsi, whom the US had chosen to support. Did any of President Obama's audience members in Cairo foresee what would soon take place in Tahrir Square? Last but not least: it was in the wake of the Cairo speech that initial signs of rebellion in Syria burgeoned into a massive uprising that faced lethal violence from the regime. The Syrian fighting quickly expanded into a proxy war between Tehran and its allies, on the one hand, and troops supported by the West (but not very well supported, one should add) on the other hand, as various Islamist groups rose simultaneously to fight both the government troops and the secular opposition.

While President Obama called for Assad to step down, the administration did very little to support the rebels. It refrained from military action of any sort: no "boots on the ground," of course, not even a "no-fly zone," and very little delivery of promised material aid. Worst of all, Washington chose to remain silent as the regime's use of chemical weapons proceeded step-by-step. Not until gas was used on a large scale, on August 21, 2013, did the president speak more boldly. He did so twice: on August 31, when he began to present the option of a military response, and on September 10, when he effectively retracted it. In the context of an ongoing civil war compounded by mass killings reminiscent of Srebrenica, these two speeches document how the president chose to refrain from offering the sort of leadership incumbent on a great power.

Future historians may eventually decipher what transpired in the Obama administration regarding Syria's chemical weapons. Did the president initially intend to set a "red line," or did he misspeak with that loaded term with its dangerous implications of the likelihood of consequences? Did Washington ever really contemplate using military force to eliminate the Syrian chemical weapons? Or was the tough posture just an effort to induce the other side to back down? Did Secretary of State John Kerry mean to open a door to arms elimination—and the Russian role—or did he speak off the cuff in ways that led to unexpected twists? The archives of the administration may eventually shed light on some of these considerations. For now, however, we are left only with the public record as we have it, and through the president's words we can trace a repeated insistence on limiting the US role in the world, in effect echoing the Cairo message of a grand withdrawal. Unlike in Cairo, however, in the two Syria speeches, the president faced a real-world crisis of mass murder. Even in the face of this crisis, however, he remained inclined to minimize the US role as much as possible. He never asks how much the

US can achieve, but rather how little it is obligated to do.

As tragic as the events in Syria have been, President Obama uses his August 31 statement to underscore that any US response will be only minimal. Certainly, he leads forcefully, stating that the gas attacks were an "assault on human dignity," they threaten our allies, and they undermine international law: grievous offenses indeed. Nonetheless, he insists that they do not warrant "boots on the ground" and that any prospective intervention will be "limited in scope and duration." The promised response seemed in no way to measure up to the gravity of the deed as described in the speech. Moreover, critics wondered about the wisdom of reassuring the enemy that an attack would be limited. Would the enemy not then just choose to wait it out?

However, the speech included a much larger limitation on military action. British Prime Minister David Cameron had just previously brought a proposal regarding a UK response to the Syria crisis to Parliament where it had been voted down, effectively precluding British participation in a campaign. (In fact, Cameron could have ignored the vote, but he announced that he chose to abide by it.) Surely the prospect of a similar legislative impasse that would stop the military action must have been on the president's mind when he decided to involve Congress. Fundamentally he was tying his hands as commander in chief, limiting his scope of military action by making it dependent on prior authorization by the Senate and the House. In the president's words: "But having made my decision as Commander-in-Chief based on what I am convinced is our national security interests, I'm also mindful that I'm the President of the world's oldest constitutional democracy. I've long believed that our power is rooted not just in our military might, but in our example as a government of the people, by the people, and for the people. And that's why I've made a second decision: I will seek authorization for the use of force from the American people's representatives in Congress." He thereby subordinated his obligation to provide for national security as commander in chief to congressional action, a particularly dubious move given the currently highly partisan and inflexible political landscape. While the president painted this decision in the idealistic colors of democratic process, it in effect placed an insurmountable limitation on the potential of US leadership. Did President Obama's motivation to go to Congress lie primarily in anticipating this opportunity to avoid action? That judgment finds support in the glaring difference between the assertion of an "assault on human dignity," which ought to have warranted prompt action, and the refusal to call Congress back from recess. The message seems to have been that grievous deeds had taken place, but they were not so tragic as to interrupt summer vacation.

This interpretation, that opting for the congressional route was at best a feint to allow for evasion, is corroborated by another twist in the narrative. On August 31 the president claimed that a debate and vote on Syria were vital to American democracy. Yet only ten days later, he called for a termination of debate before it had reached a vote. In light of the declarations of the Assad regime that it would sign on to arms control treaties and the growing engagement of Russia, matters in Syria were, he said, taking another turn. For these reasons, the democratic debate, allegedly so important in the previous speech, suddenly became superfluous, at least for the president. The rapidity with which the administration gave up on the value of the congressional path belies the initial claims of its urgent significance; Congress had been called into the process not out of principles but as a delaying tactic, and Congress can certainly delay very well.

It was, however, not only Congress that was being manipulated. Protestations to the contrary, the Syrian victims themselves were not primary on the president's mind but rather the then-still-clandestine negotiations with Iran. The endgame was not a democratization of Syria but a rapprochement with Iran. Assad's use of chemical weaponry did provide the president with an opportunity to make an indirect point to Tehran: "If we won't enforce accountability in the face of this heinous act, what does it say about our resolve to stand up to others who flout fundamental international rules? To governments who would choose to build nuclear arms? To terrorists who would spread biological weapons? To armies who carry out genocide?" He reiterated this point even more strongly on September 10: "And a failure to stand against the use of chemical weapons would weaken prohibitions against other weapons of mass destruction, and embolden Assad's ally, Iran—which must decide whether to ignore international law by building a nuclear weapon, or to take a more peaceful path." The president's focus was on Iran the entire time, even when he claimed to be speaking about Syria. Much speaks for the interpretation that, rather than ever intending to act in response to the heinous events in Syria, the president used them only to further the Iranian negotiations.

One final comparison between the two speeches supports the interpretation that the Obama administration has been systematically pursuing a reduction of the American footprint in the Middle East, giving up leadership claims, and trying, at best, to manage an orderly retreat. Even when the president correctly emphasized the extraordinary character of the Assad regime's use of chemical weapons against its own civilian population, he repeatedly coupled the expressions of condemnation with unmistakable reassurances that the US would place strict limits on its own obligations. This prospective minimization of the US involvement, interestingly, shows up in the two speeches as variations on the controversial topic of American exceptionalism.

In the August 31 speech the president, who had otherwise faced criticism for trivializing the notion of American exceptionalism, concluded with an explicit return to the exceptionalism thesis: "But we are the United States of America, and we cannot and must not turn a blind eye to what happened in Damascus. Out of the ashes of world war, we built an international order and enforced the rules that gave it meaning. And we did so because we believe that the rights of individuals to live in peace and dignity depend on the responsibilities of nations. We aren't perfect, but this nation more than any other has been willing to meet those responsibilities." America, so he argues, has built and maintained an international order because of fundamental values concerning individual rights.

The defense of these rights is the responsibility of nations, and America is exceptional because it has met this responsibility "more than others." Here, even in this his strongest statement for America's role in the world, there is no specific call for action, only an invocation to "not turn a blind eye." America must witness the crimes but apparently not necessarily act. The president cannot eschew the truism that the nation falls short of perfection. Still, one could read the statement in a more activist sense: the phrasing suggests that the US has historically exercised a leadership role for the good, and that it might continue to do so.

That activist reading is, however, not supported by the September 10 speech, in which the motif of exceptionalism returns, but in more muffled tones: "America is not the world's policeman. Terrible things happen across the globe, and it is beyond our means to right every wrong. But when, with modest effort and risk, we can stop children from being gassed to death, and thereby make our own children safer over the long run, I believe we should act. That's what makes America different. That's what makes us exceptional. With humility, but with resolve, let us never lose sight of that essential truth." The president declares that the US will not police the world and that in most situations it will not become involved. An obligation to act may apply only under very strict circumstances: in indisputable humanitarian situations, here represented by the victimization of children; where there is a plausible link to national security, implied by the condition here of making "our own children safer"; and where, at most, "modest effort and risk" are required. The Obama rhetoric is characteristically soaring, but read closely, the text places a nearly prohibitive limitation on any potential US intervention. Henceforth the world should not count on the US to provide security or guarantee an international order. America as envisioned by President Obama will not lead.

The address in Cairo and the speeches on Syria demonstrate an antipathy to American leadership. Although President Obama acknowledges that the US played a key role historically in building an international order based on peace and human dignity, he makes it clear that the US will no longer defend that order or maintain the system of allies that sustained it. The grand retreat, the withdrawal from the Middle East, is a refusal of leadership. This development is all the more striking when placed in a historical context. With the collapse of the Soviet Union, the US had emerged indisputably as the single superpower. The indispensability of US leadership had become fully evident. In that era of US predominance, Europe spread its liberal-democratic political and social systems east to areas that once belonged to the Soviet empire. Yet the bold aspirations of an expansive democratization have stalled. The Obama administration has jettisoned the democracy agenda of the Bush years. But it is not only democracy that Washington no longer promotes. It has also curtailed expectations regarding the projection of American power in general. This is the price of abandoning the mantle of leadership, since other forces quickly rush in to fill the void. The Bush administration tried to extend American influence as far east as Georgia. In contrast, the Obama administration has reduced its involvement in Central Europe, left Ukraine to Moscow, and reintroduced Russia as a major player in the Middle East. As America withdraws, Russia's status as patron of Damascus has been firmed up, and Washington's rejection of the Egyptian leadership has paved the way for Russian efforts to regain the influence in Cairo that Moscow enjoyed during the Nasser years. In November, a high-level Russian delegation, including both the foreign and defense ministers, received a warm welcome in Egypt. In December, Russia signed a twenty-five-year agreement with Syria for oil exploration off its coast. The Obama administration policies have facilitated this resurgence of Russian influence, which will only accelerate the unraveling of America's long-standing alliances.

RETREAT FROM DEMOCRACY

In addition to the retreats from politics and leadership, American withdrawal from the Middle East has also involved a retreat from democracy. There is no more stunning difference between the Bush and the Obama administrations than this. In his second inaugural address, President Bush clearly outlined an emphatic commitment to pursue democracy abroad. He grounded it in American history, ideals, and security needs: "Across the generations we have proclaimed the imperative of self-government, because no one is fit to be a master, and no one deserves to be a slave. Advancing these ideals is the mission that created our Nation. It is the honorable achievement of our fathers. Now it is the urgent requirement of our nation's security, and the calling of our time." Given those imperatives, he drew the explicit policy conclusion: "So it is the policy of the United States to seek and support the growth of democratic movements and institutions in every nation and culture, with the ultimate goal of ending tyranny in our world." As we have seen already, in Cairo President Obama explicitly distanced himself from democracy promotion: "I know there has been controversy about the promotion of democracy in recent years, and much of this controversy is connected to the war in Iraq. So let me be clear: no system of government can or should be imposed upon one nation by any other." While he continued to express his commitment "to governments that reflect the will of the people," he gave priority to the distinctiveness of different traditions. Western-style liberal democracy, so he suggested, may not be appropriate in other cultural contexts. The Bush-era universalism shattered on the Obama-era insistence of a multicultural world. The priority of culture over politics also explains why the Cairo speech thoroughly bypassed any concrete discussion of Egyptian politics and instead—ignoring political institutions and leaders—was directed to an amorphous addressee, "Muslims around the world." The message of the speech placed greater weight on religious identity than on the political rights and responsibilities of citizenship.

This diminishment of politics in the name of religion explains how weakly the Obama administration responded to the first challenge to its post-democratic policies. The reelection of Mahmoud Ahmadinejad as president of Iran, a week after the Cairo speech, provoked an enormous wave of protest. Ahmadinejad's opponents claimed widespread fraud, and by adopting the campaign color of opposition candidate

Mir Houssein Mousavi, the protests came to be known as the Green Movement. It was met with crushing violence from the police and the paramilitary Basij organization, as well as by foreign supporters of the regime, including members of Hezbollah (from Lebanon) and Hamas (from Gaza), brought in to help suppress the democracy movement. Reports circulated that arrested demonstrators faced torture and rape. Numerous fatalities occurred, and the shooting of one demonstrator, Neda Agha-Soltan, captured on video and posted to YouTube, turned her into an international cause célèbre. Because the social media played an important role in mobilizing the protests, the regime clamped down on Internet access. While support for the Green Movement spread throughout the West, the Obama administration hesitated in responding. Only belatedly did the president speak out and then only in very meek terms that never challenged the legitimacy of the election or the regime. The democratic movement in the streets of Tehran merited less US attention than did respect for the sovereignty of the Islamic Republic; the Green Movement, in the eyes of the Obama administration, did not deserve substantive American support.

The betrayal of democracy in Iran in 2009 foreshadowed the response to the rebellion against the Assad dictatorship in Syria that began in January 2011. Initially the Syrian version of the Arab Spring attracted considerable international sympathy, and even President Obama called for the end of the Assad regime. Yet the demonstrators quickly encountered violent repression. Damascus could calculate that it should imitate the success of the Tehran regime: if it could crush the protests, the international community would watch for only a little while and then forget. Yet in contrast to Iran, the Syrian uprising spiraled into a civil war between the regime and its opponents, including the West-oriented Free Syrian Army. It received verbal support from the West, especially the US, but material support was limited and slow in arriving. The rebels' disappointment with Washington has consequently grown ever more apparent. US policy has involved doing as little as possible to support democratic forces, in effect waiting for the growing number of Islamists to overwhelm the democratic opposition—in which case supporting the rebellion would become politically unpalatable—or for the Assad forces to achieve military superiority, making support for the opposition irrelevant. In other words, Washington has treated the prospects for democracy in Syria as a problem it hopes will go away, an attitude consistent with its abandonment of the Green Movement in Iran in 2009.

The reluctance to support Syrian democracy reflects the same hesitation about democratic universalism that Obama articulated in Cairo: local cultures have greater validity than human rights. The timid predisposition of the administration is to respect the legitimacy and sovereignty of existing states, as it did with Iran, no matter how brutal the character of the regime. Obama's declaration in Cairo that the US is not the world's policeman meant that he believes the US has no particular responsibility to try to influence the outcome of the Syrian conflict; hence, it has offered no more than modest verbal support for the opposition. Yet in addition to the retreat from universalism and the reluctance to challenge the sovereignty of any state, a third factor contributes to US behavior facing Syria: the dependency of Syrian sovereignty on support from Moscow. Viewed from this vantage point, US policy in Syria took shape in an important way as a function of policy toward Russia and the administration's aspiration to achieve a "reset" with Moscow after the worsening of US-Russian relations during the Bush administration. The Free Syrian Army and the democracy movement have been sacrificed to the goal of an accommodation with Russia, since Washington evidently regards Syria as part of an inviolable Russian sphere of influence. The belated and halfhearted involvement of the US in Ukraine's wavering between East and West also fits this pattern. Widespread popular sentiment to see the country move toward Western democracy through cooperation with the European Union received little endorsement from Washington, despite a stalwart last-minute appearance by Sen. John McCain who addressed the crowds in Kiev. Washington never made much effort to attract the Ukrainian government toward a Western resolution. In the end, President Viktor Yanukovych signed an agreement with Russian President Vladimir Putin, sealing a future orientation of Ukraine toward Moscow. Subsequent protests forced Yanukovych out, but the political result is unclear. The US failed to support the democratic movement strongly.

Only in one instance has US policy appeared to value democracy, though in a peculiarly limited manner: Egypt, where the twists of recent history have been particularly complex. On January 25, 2011, as protests grew against the rule of Mubarak, President Obama signaled that he no longer supported the ally of decades. After Mubarak stepped down on February 11, the military assumed power but prepared the way for national elections that took place between November 2011 and February 2012. Islamist groups, especially the Muslim Brotherhood, swept to victory in the Parliament. In a runoff election for the presidency in June 2012, Muslim Brotherhood candidate Mohamed Morsi won with 51.7 percent of the vote against Ahmed Shafiq, who had served as the last prime minister under Mubarak and who received 48.3 percent with an overall 52 percent participation rate. A new era seemed to have begun, but Egypt remained deeply divided. Despite the close outcome, Morsi pursued strident policies as if he had an overwhelming mandate, centralizing ever more power in his office and protecting his decisions from any judicial review: Morsi would be above the law. Protests against Morsi and the Muslim Brotherhood began to mushroom, quickly mobilizing millions by June 30. After issuing an ultimatum, the military deposed Morsi, arresting him along with other leaders of the Muslim Brotherhood. Violent demonstrations for and against Morsi filled the streets of Egyptian cities. The anti-Morsi public widely embraced the military takeover, and General Abdel Fattah el-Sisi emerged as the leading figure in Egyptian politics and an object of popular adulation.

Despite these complexities, the US defense of democracy in Egypt has been restricted to an inflexible support for Morsi as the electoral victor in 2012. This understanding of democracy is narrowly majoritarian and procedural, be-cause it leaves out of consideration the extensive restrictions against democratic procedure the Morsi government was putting into place.

In other words, America's ostensible support for democracy in Egypt has depended on an extremely limited understanding of democracy as exclusively about the vote count, without consideration of Morsi's destruction of liberal-democratic institutions. This suggests that US policy in Egypt does not represent a fundamental exception to the rule we have seen played out: the abandonment of democracy in Iran and Syria. In Cairo, the US has similarly managed to position itself against the popular democratic forces that were outraged by Morsi's encroachments on liberal procedures and democratic rights. Therefore in Egypt, too, has the Obama administration pursued a policy of retreat from democracy. The administration has been consistent on that point. It's no wonder it has been prepared to see relations with the one functioning democracy in the region, Israel, deteriorate significantly.

Pulling back from the democratic aspirations of the past, the Obama administration has been fundamentally revising the mission of the US and its role in the Middle East. Because the US cannot be counted on as an advocate for democracy and rule of law, a profound shift has begun to unfold in the region. Because the US has abandoned its historic commitment to the universalism of liberal modernity, democratic forces—in Iran, Syria, and Egypt—are no longer looking as much toward Washington. Of course the region has its own indigenous capacity for democracy, as evidenced by the Arab Spring and the masses of demonstrators and rebels. Yet as the US responds to cries for democracy only with callous apathy, political actors have begun to make new calculations. Dwindling US commitment to the politics of the region and an abdication of leadership for democratic change leave space for new powers to emerge and compete: the regional aspirations of Turkey, the rising star of a hegemonic and nuclear Iran, and the cold hand of Putinist Russia rebuilding the lost Soviet empire.

There is a price to pay for the grand retreat. Whatever its motivations, whether driven by a changing American culture or the particular preferences of the Obama administration, US withdrawal from the region could have long-term consequences, as other forces come forward to fill the vacuum. Yet the withdrawal is not a foregone conclusion. The American political landscape may change, and a new administration could pursue different policy options. While it is true that large parts of the American public grew weary of the wars in Afghanistan and Iraq, the president has not been making the case for the importance of either campaign. More importantly, in response to the democracy movements in the Middle East—in Tehran, Damascus, and Cairo—the American public responded spontaneously with a high degree of sympathy. As a nation, our deepest allegiances always belong to peoples struggling for freedom. How to translate that popular sentiment into effective policy could be the challenge of the next president, part of a quest to reestablish America's leadership in international politics in the pursuit of democratic ideals.

ABOUT THE AUTHOR

Russell A. Berman, the Walter A. Haas Professor in the Humanities at Stanford University, is a senior fellow at the Hoover Institution and a member of the Herbert and Jane Dwight Working Group on Islamism and the International Order. He specializes in German culture and is a member of both the Department of German Studies and the Department of Comparative Literature at Stanford University. Professor Berman is the author of numerous articles and books including *Enlightenment or Empire: Colonial Discourse in German Culture* (1998) and *The Rise of the Modern German Novel: Crisis and Charisma* (1986), both of which won the Outstanding Book Award of the German Studies Association. Other books include *Anti-Americanism in Europe: A*

Cultural Problem (2004), *Fiction Sets You Free: Literature, Liberty and Western Culture* (2007), and, most recently, *Freedom or Terror: Europe Faces Jihad* (2010).

HERBERT AND JANE DWIGHT
WORKING GROUP ON
ISLAMISM AND THE
INTERNATIONAL ORDER

THE HERBERT AND JANE DWIGHT WORKING
GROUP ON ISLAMISM AND THE INTERNATIONAL
ORDER seeks to engage in the task of reversing Islamic radicalism through reforming and strengthening the legitimate role of the state across the entire Muslim world. Efforts will draw on the intellectual resources of an array of scholars and practitioners from within the United States and abroad, to foster the pursuit of modernity, human flourishing, and the rule of law and reason in Islamic lands—developments that are critical to the very order of the international system.

The Working Group is cochaired by Hoover fellows Fouad Ajami and Charles Hill, with an active participation by Hoover Institution Director John Raisian. Current core membership includes Russell A. Berman and Abbas Milani, with contributions from Zeyno Baran, Marius Deeb, Reuel Marc Gerecht, Ziad Haider, R. John Hughes, Nibras Kazimi, Bernard Lewis, Habib C. Malik, Camille Pecastaing, Itamar Rabinovich, Lieutenant Colonel Joel Rayburn, Lee Smith, Samuel Tadros, Joshua Teitelbaum, and Tunku Varadarajan.

[For a list of essays published under the auspices of the
WORKING GROUP ON ISLAMISM AND THE INTERNATIONAL ORDER,
please see page ii.]

INDEX